Dear Parents and Educators,

Welcome to Penguin Young Readers! As parents and educators, you know that each child develops at his or her own pace—in terms of speech, critical thinking, and, of course, reading. Penguin Young Readers recognizes this fact. As a result, each Penguin Young Readers book is assigned a traditional easy-to-read level (1–4) as well as a Guided Reading Level (A–P). Both of these systems will help you choose the right book for your child. Please refer to the back of each book for specific leveling information. Penguin Young Readers features esteemed authors and illustrators, stories about favorite characters, fascinating nonfiction, and more!

Butterflies

LEVEL 2

GUIDED READING LEVEL **I**

This book is perfect for a **Progressing Reader** who:
- can figure out unknown words by using picture and context clues;
- can recognize beginning, middle, and ending sounds;
- can make and confirm predictions about what will happen in the text; and
- can distinguish between fiction and nonfiction.

Here are some **activities** you can do during and after reading this book:
- Nonfiction: Nonfiction books deal with facts and events that are real. Talk about the elements of nonfiction. Discuss some of the facts you learned about butterflies. Then, on a separate sheet of paper, write down the steps it takes for a butterfly egg to turn into a butterfly.
- Compare/Contrast: Moths and butterflies might look alike, but they are different. Discuss how they are alike and how they are different.

Remember, sharing the love of reading with a child is the best gift you can give!

—Bonnie Bader, EdM
   Penguin Young Readers program

*Penguin Young Readers are leveled by independent reviewers applying the standards developed by Irene Fountas and Gay Su Pinnell in *Matching Books to Readers: Using Leveled Books in Guided Reading*, Heinemann, 1999.

For Mom & Dad—EBN

In memory of Katelyn Webb.
We will forever cherish that special closeness
and the cuddles shared while reading
books together—Love, Mom & Dad

Penguin Young Readers
Published by the Penguin Group
Penguin Group (USA) Inc., 375 Hudson Street, New York, New York 10014, USA
Penguin Group (Canada), 90 Eglinton Avenue East, Suite 700, Toronto, Ontario M4P 2Y3, Canada
(a division of Pearson Penguin Canada Inc.)
Penguin Books Ltd., 80 Strand, London WC2R 0RL, England
Penguin Group Ireland, 25 St. Stephen's Green, Dublin 2, Ireland (a division of Penguin Books Ltd.)
Penguin Group (Australia), 250 Camberwell Road, Camberwell, Victoria 3124, Australia
(a division of Pearson Australia Group Pty. Ltd.)
Penguin Books India Pvt. Ltd., 11 Community Centre, Panchsheel Park, New Delhi—110 017, India
Penguin Group (NZ), 67 Apollo Drive, Rosedale, Auckland 0632, New Zealand
(a division of Pearson New Zealand Ltd.)
Penguin Books (South Africa) (Pty.) Ltd., 24 Sturdee Avenue,
Rosebank, Johannesburg 2196, South Africa

Penguin Books Ltd., Registered Offices: 80 Strand, London WC2R 0RL, England

Text copyright © 2000 by Emily Neye. Illustrations copyright © 2000 by Ron Broda.
All rights reserved. First published in 2000 by Grosset & Dunlap, an imprint of Penguin Group (USA) Inc.
Published in 2012 by Penguin Young Readers, an imprint of Penguin Group (USA) Inc.,
345 Hudson Street, New York, New York 10014. Manufactured in China.

Library of Congress Control Number: 00025925

ISBN 978-0-448-41966-4   10 9 8 7 6 5 4 3 2

Butterflies

by Emily Neye
illustrated by Ron Broda

Penguin Young Readers
An Imprint of Penguin Group (USA) Inc.

Butterflies live

all over the world.

They are in backyard gardens.

They are in
rainforests far away.

You can find butterflies

on cold mountains . . .

and in hot deserts.

Butterflies are insects

like flies and ladybugs.

They have six legs,

a body in three parts,

and skin that is hard like a shell.

Like most insects,

butterflies have wings.

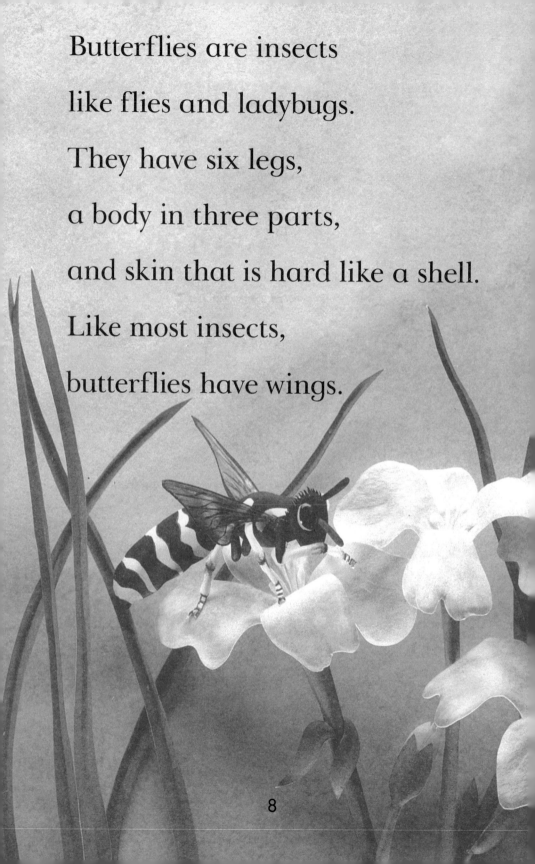

There are more than
20,000 kinds
of butterflies.
They come in
all different colors.

Butterflies come

in different sizes.

The biggest butterfly has wings

as wide as a robin's wings.

The smallest butterfly

is about the size

of this picture.

But every butterfly
starts out the same way—

as a tiny egg.

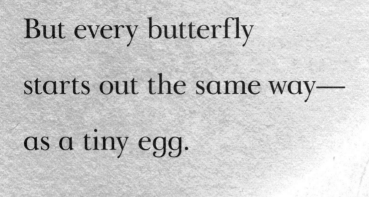

This monarch (say: MON-ark)
butterfly has just laid
one of her eggs on a leaf.

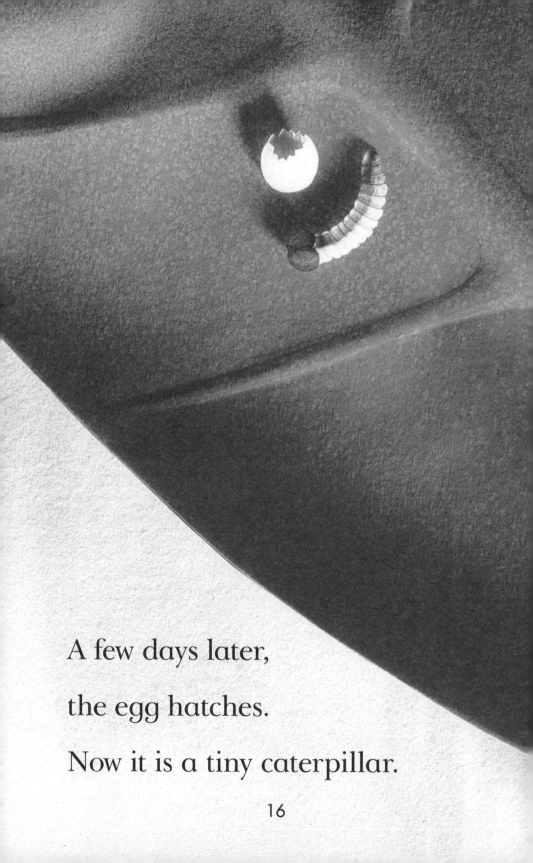

A few days later,

the egg hatches.

Now it is a tiny caterpillar.

All the caterpillar does is

eat and rest,

eat and rest.

It chews up many leaves.

It grows and grows.

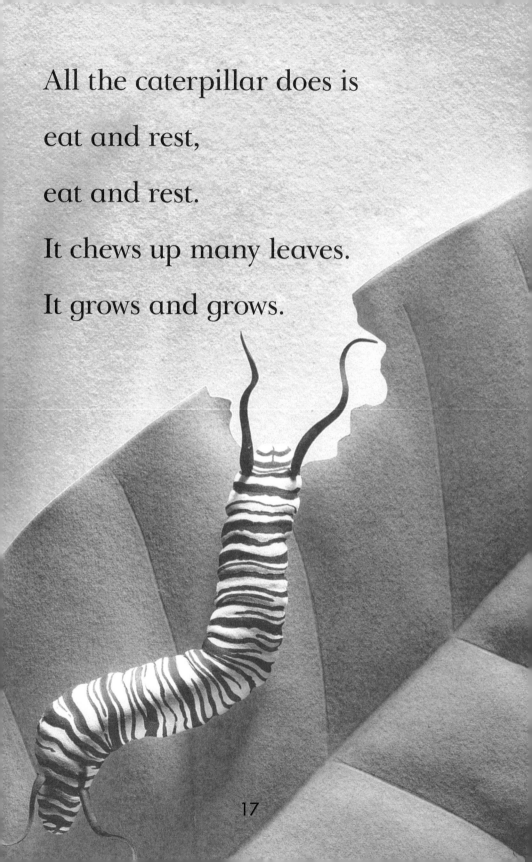

Two weeks go by.

Now the caterpillar

is ready to change.

It finds a safe spot

on a twig or leaf.

It spins a silk pad.

It hangs down from the pad.

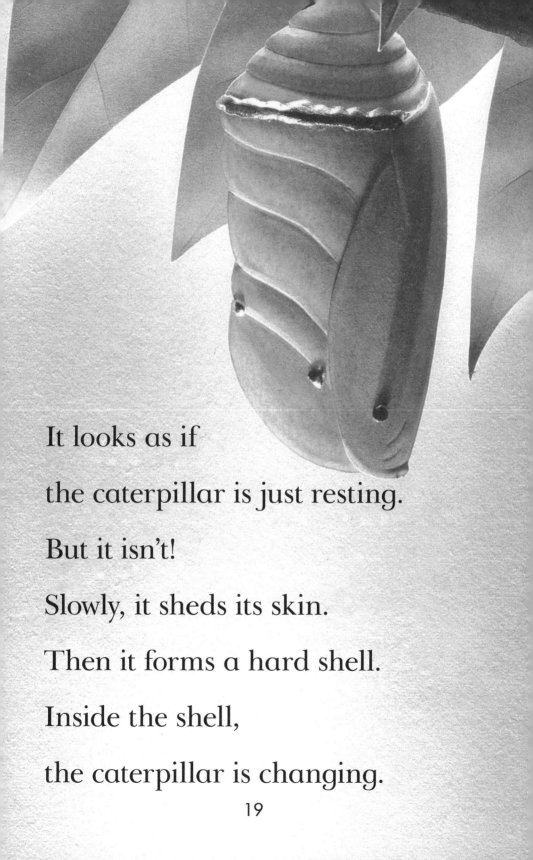

It looks as if

the caterpillar is just resting.

But it isn't!

Slowly, it sheds its skin.

Then it forms a hard shell.

Inside the shell,

the caterpillar is changing.

After about a week,

the shell cracks open.

Out comes a pretty

monarch butterfly!

Her wings are wet.

She can't fly yet.

She must let her wings

dry in the sun.

Then the monarch flies

to a bed of flowers.

She is hungry.

Butterflies do not eat leaves

like caterpillars.

They suck sweet juices

from flowers.

Their tongues work like straws.

Some animals like
to eat butterflies.

But these butterflies are safe.

Their wings look like
leaves and bark.

This bird does not see them.

Can you see them?

Are these butterflies?

No. They are moths.

Moths look a lot like butterflies.

But they fly at night.

Butterflies fly in the daytime.

Is this a butterfly?

Yes!

You can tell

because its wings

are closed.

When a moth rests,

its wings stay open.

27

The summer is ending.

Fall is on the way.

Most butterflies do not like the cold.

Some sleep all winter.

They find quiet spots,

such as a cave or your attic.

Other butterflies fly south
to warm places.

Monarch butterflies

fly many, many miles.

Clouds of them fill the sky.

In the spring,

they fly back north.

There, they will lay

their eggs.

And soon,

new butterflies will be here.

Maybe some will be

in your backyard!